Oscar's Day

By Jenny Vaughan and Cynthia Benjamin

CELEBRATION PRESS
Pearson Learning Group

Meet Oscar. He is nine years old.
Oscar lives on a farm in Bolivia.
His village is in the mountains.

Today Oscar and his family
are going to the market.

South
America

Bolivia

Bolivia is a country in South America.

Oscar can't walk to the market.
It is too far from his house.
The market is an hour away by bus.

Oscar's house is made from clay and straw bricks.

Oscar wakes up early on market day.
"Before we go, I must help Mama
on the farm," he says. "First, I help
plant potatoes."

Oscar's family grows
potatoes.

◄ This is Oscar's mother.
He calls her Mama.

Next, Oscar feeds the farm animals. Sheep, pigs, cows, chickens, and rabbits live on Oscar's farm. "I like the rabbits best," says Oscar.

This calf lives on Oscar's farm. Her name is Lila.

When the farm work is done, it is finally time to go to the market. Oscar and his brother and cousin wear sweaters, vests, and hats to stay warm.

Efrain is Oscar's brother. Rodrigo is their cousin.

Efrain

Oscar

Rodrigo

Oscar and his family take the bus to the market. "The market is fun to see," says Oscar. His family brings home many good things to eat.

Oscar's family buys vegetables and rice at the market. Rice is Oscar's favorite food.